Police on Policing

The Unsung Consensus

Candid Conversations on the State of Law Enforcement in America

---

By Sheriff Alfonzo Williams
Edited by Ty Hager

DEDICATION

To the brave men and women of Law Enforcement, and to all those whom they serve and protect.

Police on Policing

The Unsung Consensus

All rights reserved. No portion of this book may be reproduced mechanically, electronically, or by any other means, including photocopying, without written permission of the author. It is illegal to copy the book, post it to a website, or distribute it by any other means without permission from the author.

Copyright © 2020 Alfonzo Williams

All rights reserved.

Table of Contents

Introduction 1

The Experts.. 8

The Lingo 28

Chapter One: Raising The Bar: Education,
Training, And Screening 31

Chapter Two: Trust, Transparency, And Body Cams..................... 42

Chapter Three: Too Many Chiefs In The Kitchen
Jurisdictional Issues 47

Chapter Four: Guardians, Warriors, And Servants 51

Chapter Five: Strained Bedfellows: Politics
And Policing.. 56

Chapter Six: Long Arm, Helping Hand
Law Enforcement And The Community.. 63

Chapter Seven: Use Of Force 69

Chapter Eight: Racism.. 77

Chapter Nine: Do As I Say And As I Do
The Role Of Leadership In Law Enforcement 84

Chapter Ten: Moving Forward: What Does
Law Enforcement Reform Look Like? 89

My Letter To Governor Kemp 96

Acknowledgements..100

About The Author..102

INTRODUCTION

My name's Alfonzo Williams. I've been a dedicated peace officer for thirty years, rising from patrol officer to detective to police chief to sheriff (I was recently elected – with 85% of the vote – to my second term as sheriff of Burke County, Georgia), along the way becoming a certified instructor and heading up two police academies.

When I look back on the history of policing in America during my life and career, it seems that everything changed on April 29th, 1992.

I'd been accustomed to an element of mistrust for law enforcement among some in the Black community. Raised in poverty (one of seven kids brought up by our single mother) in Burke's county seat of Waynesboro, I had seen it in my own neighborhood. As an African-American police officer in nearby Augusta, I'd been called everything from an "Uncle Tom" to worse. It was just something that went with the badge, and those who distrusted us were still by-and-large only a small fraction of the public.

That percentage grew considerably, and began crossing racial demographics, with the video of those officers beating the hell out of Rodney King in 1991. The "not guilty" verdict almost a year to the day afterward was, I believe, the tipping point.

As I recount in my recent memoirs, "Not Here To Be Served," I'd just turned 21, but had already risen to the position of FTO (Field Training Officer) in the APD. On April 29th, 1992, I got a call from dispatch to go to a predominantly-Black housing project regarding a reported assault of a juvenile by an adult. When my junior officer and I arrived, the victim's mother pointed out the assailant, an African-American male sitting with a group of other Black men under a shade tree.

"Man, we're already pissed off about the Rodney King verdict," one said when we asked about the assault on the minor. "Don't come over here with that bullshit!"

We hadn't heard about the verdict and said so. We added that it had absolutely *nothing* to do with why we were there.

The situation escalated, back-up was called, and a near-riot ensued, calm finally restored by a Remington shotgun fired into the air by another officer. None of us knew that - at that moment in cities all across the country - much more deadly riots were breaking out, from the ashes of which would arise a fundamental shift in the way the public viewed police and policing.

That's my opinion, anyway.

Things didn't really change much over the next two decades or so, as a whole new generation was raised to view law enforcement as almost the lesser of two evils. Sometimes *not* the lesser. Gone was the near-universal respectful and trustful regard in which my chosen field had been held throughout most of human history. When, as a young boy, I'd dreamed of becoming a police officer, it was in large part because I wanted to be known as one of the *good* guys.

Systemically, we had twenty years to address the issues which had so tarnished our profession but seemed to instead fall into complacency. Perhaps change was so difficult because the broader issues are so complex, a myriad of practicalities wrapped in concepts and unfortunate truths of basic human behavior. Maybe we were just glad it wasn't getting worse.

In 2014, in the city of Ferguson, Missouri, it got worse.

If the stretch of time between the L.A. riots and the shooting of the young, Black, and unarmed Michael Brown could be called a plateau for law enforcement in America, the succession of downward steps – from Eric Garner to Tamir Rice, Freddie Gray, Sandra Bland, Philando Castle, and ultimately to George Floyd in Minneapolis – has been a virtual nosedive into disgrace. If one were to judge us based upon news reports and social media posts, one would think we were the enemy: A heavily-armed gang of government-sanctioned bullies, racists, and psychopaths with itchy trigger fingers and hardened hearts.

While neither I or *any* law enforcement professionals I know discount the veracity or seriousness of the vast majority of these cases, to paint our entire *profession* with the same brush as the perpetrators of these crimes requires the exact level of prejudice as that of which we are so cavalierly accused.

If you'll pardon my grammar, *it just ain't right.*

However, we as law enforcement professionals are not tasked with fixing fundamental human flaws. People are going to make ill-conceived judgments and have convenient misperceptions; to seek truth requires a mind open enough to receive it and – oftentimes – a modicum of *effort*. As a society, we're becoming less and less inclined toward either.

What we *can* do – collectively, as the overwhelming majority of dedicated law enforcement professionals to whom our careers are not just jobs but *callings* – is acknowledge and address the issues which have led us here and, through commitment and transparency, demonstrate that we hear the voices for reform and *wholeheartedly agree*.

That's what this book is about.

Shortly after the George Floyd murder, I wrote a letter to the governor of Georgia, outlining steps I think are necessary to repair a dysfunctional system and begin the journey toward repairing a badly-damaged public trust. Included in the steps:

- Requiring 4-year degrees for all law enforcement officers
- Setting national standards for certification and training, including ongoing mental screenings and exhaustive background checks
- Creating a national retirement system for law-enforcement
- Providing the funding necessary to make *real* change possible and transform law enforcement into a respected profession and not just a "job"

I realized that I could do more than just write letters. I knew from talking with my fellow law enforcement leaders (and this is a dialogue which has been ongoing through the decades) that we were on the same page about the vast majority of issues, and that we were on the same page as the *public* on far more than they knew. I believe – *we* believe – that one great step toward establishing trust is simply by communicating.

Police on Policing: The Unsung Consensus is – basically – a bunch of law enforcement veterans talking about law enforcement in America in

2020. We're a collection of current and former sheriffs and police chiefs and chief deputies and teachers and writers, all first-and-foremost dedicated public servants and peace officers. Even more than that, we're just like *you*.

Through a series of Zoom meetings and email correspondences, we discussed what's wrong, how it *went* wrong, and – in our professional opinions – ways we can work together to make it right again. We don't agree on every single issue but, as you'll read, we don't disagree on much. We also, hopefully, shed some insight into what it's like to be in law enforcement, what it takes to become a police officer, and help to dispel some harmful and unwarranted myths.

Sir Robert Peel, who in 1829 founded the London Metropolitan Police Force and became known as the "Father of Policing," gave every new cadet in his agency a copy of his *Principles of Policing*. As you read the discussions I had with my law enforcement brethren, I think you'll find that these principles – which form the foundation of "policing by consent" - are as valid and relevant as ever.

Peel's Principles:

1. To prevent crime and disorder, as an alternative to their repression by military force and severity of legal punishment.

2. To recognize always that the power of the police to fulfill their functions and duties is dependent on public approval of their existence, actions, and behavior, and on their ability to secure and maintain public respect.

3. To recognize always that to secure and maintain the respect and approval of the public means also the securing of the willing co-operation of the public in the task of securing observance of laws.

4. To recognize always that the extent to which the co-operation of the public can be secured diminishes proportionately the necessity of the use of physical force and compulsion for achieving police objectives.

5. To seek and preserve public favor, not by pandering to public opinion, but by constantly demonstrating absolutely impartial service to law, in complete independence of policy, and without regard to the justice or injustice of the substance of individual laws, by ready offering of individual service and friendship to all members of the public without regard to their wealth or social standing, by ready exercise of courtesy and friendly good humor, and by ready offering of individual sacrifice in protecting and preserving life.

6. To use physical force only when the exercise of persuasion, advice and warning is found to be insufficient to obtain public co-operation to an extent necessary to secure observance of law or to restore order, and to use only the minimum degree of physical force which is necessary on any particular occasion for achieving a police objective.

7. To maintain at all times a relationship with the public that gives reality to the historic tradition that the police are the public and that the public are the police, the police being only members of the public who are paid to give full-time attention to duties which are incumbent on every citizen in the interests of community welfare and existence.

8. To recognize always the need for strict adherence to police-executive functions, and to refrain from even seeming to usurp the powers of the judiciary of avenging individuals or the State, and of authoritatively judging guilt and punishing the guilty.

9. To recognize always that the test of police efficiency is the absence of crime and disorder, and not the visible evidence of police action in dealing with them.

THE EXPERTS

While it's not particularly difficult to *become* a police officer (more on that in the next chapter), it takes a tremendous amount of hard work and dedication to rise through the ranks to become a law enforcement *leader*. We certainly don't do it for the money (more on that later too), we don't do it for accolades (those are few and far between), and we don't do it for the power. Those who rise in our profession only do so by realizing that the *true* power lies within the communities we serve. As the second of Peel's Principles states: *To recognize always that the power of the police to fulfill their functions and duties is dependent on public approval of their existence, actions, and behavior, and on their ability to secure and maintain public respect.*

This principle is woven into the DNA of almost every law enforcement leader I've ever known, and the panel we assembled for *Police on Policing* is no exception. Many of our experts are old friends, including a couple I actually trained. Some are new friends, referred either by the *Law Enforcement Action Partnership* (LEAP) or Dean Crisp - who also participated in the forum) - through his *Leaders Helping Leaders Network* (LHLN).

Most of our panel are from the southern states, but we also have representation from New York, Ohio, and Minnesota. Apart from the subject of the influence of police unions (northern states have them, southern states don't), the issues we discussed are pretty universal.

JERRY BLASH

A 25-year veteran of law enforcement and corrections, Jerry has been a Deputy Chief of Police, Investigations Commander, Vice and Narcotics Supervisor, Patrol Supervisor, Field Training Officer, Internal Affairs Commander, School Resource Commander, Jail Security Manager, Academy Adjunct Instructor, and Department Training Officer. I actually had the honor of being one of Jerry's instructors, and he likes to tell people he knew me when I had hair.

Currently the Chief of Police of Walthourville, Georgia, Jerry is also (for the past decade) a Senior Instructor for the *Peace Officer Standards and Training Council* (POST), and holds a Bachelor's Degree in Criminal Justice from Saint Leo University, and a Master's Degree in Justice Administration from Faulkner University.

While he didn't grow up dreaming of becoming a police officer, Jerry says, "I knew I wanted to do something positive. My family has a history of drugs and alcohol…just low education and that type of thing. Out of my immediate family, I was the first one to graduate from college, and I'm probably the only one who hasn't been arrested."

Jerry is a member of the Georgia Association of Chiefs of Police, Southern States Police Benevolent Association, Peace Officers Annuity

Benefit Fund, and the Georgia Internal Affairs Investigators Association.

WILLIE BURLEY

In law enforcement since 1991, Willie started out at the Burke County Sheriff's Office around the same time I was going to the police academy in Augusta. He's been an officer for several police departments, headed up the BCSO's Community Services division, and was police chief for Stapleton, Georgia. Currently, Willie's chief of the Waynesboro PD, so I have the honor of working with him on a regular basis.

DEAN CRISP

After briefly playing Major League baseball, Dean began his law enforcement career in 1977 as a police dispatcher in Asheville, North Carolina. He quickly rose through the ranks, becoming a Captain at 29.

A former police chief for the cities of Greer and Columbia, South Carolina, Dean is currently a faculty member of the FBI Law Enforcement Executive Development Association, a national instructor for the Carolinas Institute for Community Policing, and has an Associate of Arts Degree in Criminal Justice, Bachelor of Science Degree in Criminal Justice and a Master's in Public Affairs from Western Carolina University. He's also a consultant for The Institute for Intergovernmental Research in Tallahassee, Florida and is the founder and president of Crisp Consulting and the Leaders Helping Leaders Network, based in Asheville.

In his book, *Leadership Lessons from the Thin Blue Line*, Dean says, "Since my early days as a kid, I have had a strong desire to help others. It feels like it is in my DNA. It makes me get up in the morning and keeps me going."

In 1983, Dean received the Thomas Jefferson Award from the American

Institute for Public Service for his work with disadvantaged youth.

BILLY HANCOCK

Billy is a 44-year veteran of Public Safety, serving his home of Crisp County, Georgia for most of his career. Beginning as an EMT in 1976, he was sworn in as a part-time deputy with the Crisp County Sheriff's Office in 1979. Following a stint with the Georgia State Patrol, he returned to CCSO and later spent 19 years as Chief Deputy. He's currently not only in his sixth year as Crisp County Sheriff, but also director of the county's Emergency Management agency.

Hancock is an avid public speaker, conducting educational and motivational speeches to local clubs, schools, and businesses. He has also lectured throughout the United States and Canada on various law enforcement topics for the Drug Enforcement Administration and St. Petersburg Junior College. A graduate of the Moultrie Technical College EMS Program and the Georgia State Patrol Academy, he also has an Associate degree in Criminal Justice and a Master Certificate in Emergency Management, along with multiple Instructor certifications for various specialty courses dealing with law enforcement. He's a board member of Georgia's POST, past Vice-President of the Georgia Peace Officers Association and is an active member of both the Georgia and National Sheriff's Associations. He continues to teach on the State and Federal levels.

Sadly, Billy's wife Mary Ellen passed away during the writing of this book, and his participation was limited. I greatly appreciate the insight and wisdom he was able to provide, and my prayers remain with he and his family.

WAYNE HARRIS

Wayne began his law enforcement career in 1987 as a patrol officer with the Rochester Police Department in New York, working his way up through sergeant, captain, commander, and finally to deputy chief. He's been a liaison between the police and street gangs, investigated police misconduct, and – prior to his retirement in 2017 - set up a police training advisory committee. Wayne is the recipient of multiple citations and awards, is a member of the board of LEAP, and serves as Chief Financial Office of NOBLE, the National Association of Black Law Enforcement Executive*s*. He holds a B.S. in Organizational Management from Roberts Wesleyan College and is a graduate of the F.B.I. National Academy.

Wayne writes and lectures extensively about police/community relations, implicit bias, and procedural justice.

RAMONE LAMKIN

Ramone began his career in law enforcement nearly a quarter-century ago with the Richmond County Sheriff's Office in Augusta, Georgia. In 2002, he became a trooper for the Georgia State Patrol, where he reached the rank of corporal and was made an assistant post commander.

Returning to RCSO in 2012 as division commander of the Traffic Safety Division, Ramone was elected the county's marshal in 2016.

A graduate of the FBI National Academy, Ramone also holds both bachelor's and master's degrees in Criminal Justice.

HOBART LEWIS

For Hobart, law enforcement is in the blood. He grew up wanting to wear a badge, as his father did for both the Greenville, South Carolina Police Department, and the Greenville County Sheriff's Office.

"Law enforcement has always been a part of my life and I have always had an interest in serving my community through a law enforcement capacity," he says.

Hobart joined the Greenville PD in 1994, serving as a patrolman, corporal, sergeant, and tactical team commander, then later went to work for the sheriff's office. In March of 2020, he was elected sheriff in a special election (garnering 75% of the vote).

JIM MANFRE

Jim, who is also a practicing attorney, began his law enforcement career as an investigator for the Bronx District Attorney's Office Major Offense Bureau and was assistant DA for New York's Suffolk County, where he prosecuted violent felony, child abuse, and even mob cases.

Growing up in both New York and Florida, Jim retired to the Sunshine State to pursue real estate development, but was once again drawn to law enforcement, elected as sheriff of Flagler County from 2001-2005 and from 2012-2016. As sheriff, he transformed the county's 275-person agency with new personnel training, computer systems, and crime monitoring practices, initiating community-policing and youth programs and becoming one of the first sheriffs in Florida to fully implement body cams in his patrol division, all of which led to significant reductions in crime under his watch.

Jim is currently an acting attorney, real estate developer, and LEAP lecturer.

EARLE MARSH

Earle began his career in 1991, writing parking tickets for the Columbia Police Department in South Carolina. Following six years on patrol, nine years in Narcotics (where he was a part of the FBI and DEA task forces), and a stint as a canine handler, he was promoted to Sergeant and assigned to the Community Response Team, then to Lieutenant and made Watch Commander. In his current role as Columbia PD's Special Operations Captain, Earle oversees multiple units, including SWAT and Crisis Negotiations.

CHARLES PRESCOTT

One of the "youngsters" of our group, Charles has packed a lot of law enforcement experience into his 13 years and emerged as a leader in public safety in Georgia. Beginning as a Juvenile Corrections Officer for the GA Department of Juvenile Justice, Charles quickly worked his way to the Burke County Sheriff's Office then to the Waynesboro Police Department, where – as police chief (this was in 2011) – I hired him to lead our Narcotics/Vice and Violent Crimes investigations.

Upon my departure from the Waynesboro PD in 2013, Charles sought out his own greener pastures and helped establish the first-ever police department at Augusta's Paine College, where he served as Assistant Police Chief. In 2014, he was named the Assistant Chief Investigator for the Fulton County (Atlanta) DA's Office and – in November of 2019 – became the Chief Criminal Investigator in the Cobb County (Marietta) DA's Office.

A certified POST instructor, Charles also has a bachelor's degree in Sociology and master's degrees in both Emergency Management and Biblical Counseling.

I knew he'd go far.

THOMAS SMITH

Thomas joined the St. Paul, Minnesota PD in 1989, working "every single position" in his climb up the ladder to Police Chief, a post he held from 2010-2016. At the beginning of his term heading the department, he hung a quote by Martin Luther King, Jr. - which Thomas says has guided him throughout his life and career – on his wall:

"The ultimate measure of a man is not where he stands in moments of comfort and convenience, but where he stands at times of challenge and controversy."

As a biracial kid growing up on St. Paul's West Side, Thomas says he "didn't have a healthy respect for law enforcement or the police at that time, because on a few occasions I'd been stopped by the police or brought home and/or thrown on the hood of a squad car." His perspective and life direction changed when "a couple of officers took the time to really talk to me."

Thomas is a graduate of the of the FBI National Academy, the Law Enforcement Executive Development Seminar (LEEDS), the FBI National Executive Institute, and the International Leadership in Counter-Terrorism program. He holds a bachelor's degree in Public Relations from Metropolitan State University and master's degree in

Leadership and Education from St. Thomas University.

TOM THOMPSON

Thompson began his law enforcement career in 1995 as a patrol officer with the Miamisburg Police Department in Ohio and went on to serve as the department's Assistant Police Chief. Beginning in 2018, he took up his current position as Network Executive Director of Police with the Kettering Health Network. He's a member of the Montgomery County Improving Modern Police and Community Trust, the International Association of Hospital Safety and Security, the International Association of Chiefs of Police, as well as several other state and local police chiefs' associations.

TOMMIE WALKER

Tommie is another peace officer whom I've had the pleasure of knowing throughout his career. He began with the Burke County Sheriff's Office in 2003 and spent nearly fifteen years with the department before he became Police Chief of Wadley, Georgia in 2018 – the position he currently holds.

A tireless proponent of community involvement, Tommie recently facilitated a forum entitled "Know Your Rights and the Law: What You Should Know When Encountered by the Police."

JOHN T. WILCHER

A veteran with 44 years of service with the Chatham County Sheriff's Office (Savannah, GA), Sheriff John T. Wilcher has served in nearly every capacity of law enforcement. A recipient of the Georgia Sheriffs' Association *Excellence Award*, his office last year became the first in the country to be accredited for mental health services as well as the first to achieve dual accreditation in mental health and health services from the National Commission on Correctional Health Care (NCCHC).

THE LINGO

Below are a few of the law enforcement terms, phrases, and acronyms used throughout.

CALEA

The Commission on Accreditation for Law Enforcement Agencies, Inc. was created in 1979 as a credentialing authority through the joint efforts of law enforcement's major executive associations. The CALEA Accreditation program seals are reserved for use by those public safety agencies that have demonstrated compliance with CALEA Standards and have been awarded CALEA Accreditation by the Commission. At this time in law enforcement, it's pretty much the accreditation standard.

FIELD TRAINING

Training which takes place outside of the academy, usually on patrol. Supervised by a Field Training Officer (FTO).

GRAHAM VS CONNOR

Graham v. Connor, 490 U.S. 386 (1989), was a United States Supreme

Court case where the Court determined that an objective reasonableness standard should apply to a civilian's claim that law enforcement officials used excessive force in the course of making an arrest, investigatory stop, or other "seizure" of his person. In short, the ruling says that the standard for use of force is what a "reasonable" officer would do in such circumstances.

MMPI

The Minnesota Multiphasic Personality Inventory is a standardized psychometric test of adult personality and psychopathology. Psychologists and other mental health professionals use various versions of the MMPI to help develop treatment plans, assist with differential diagnosis, help answer legal questions (forensic psychology), screen job candidates during the personnel selection process, or as part of a therapeutic assessment procedure.

PIT MANEUVER

The PIT maneuver (or TVI) is a pursuit tactic by which a pursuing car can force a fleeing car to turn sideways abruptly, causing the driver to lose control and stop. Other names include *pit block*, *pit stop*, and *blocking*. It was developed and named by the Fairfax County Police Department of Virginia, United States. Other interpretations of the acronym "PIT" include *pursuit immobilization technique*, *precision immobilization technique*, *push it tough*, *parallel immobilization technique*, and *precision intervention tactic*. The technique is also known as *tactical car intervention*, *tactical ramming*, *legal intervention*, and *fishtailing*.

POST

Peace Officer Standards and Training or Police Officers Standards and Training is more commonly known as POST. POST is a board or council of people appointed by the Governor to set the minimum educational requirements for police officers. Currently, every U.S. state except Hawaii has a version of POST or its equivalent.

21st CENTURY POLICING

The President's Task Force on 21st Century Policing was created by an executive order signed by President Barack Obama on December 18, 2014. Obama created it in response to the unrest in Ferguson, Missouri following the shooting of Michael Brown by a police officer there. The eleven members of the task force included academics, law enforcement officials, and civil rights activists.

USE OF FORCE CONTINUUM

A use of force continuum is a standard that provides law enforcement officers and civilians with guidelines as to how much force may be used against a resisting subject in a given situation. In some ways, it is similar to the U.S. military's escalation of force (EOF). The purpose of these models is to clarify, both for law enforcement officers and civilians, the complex subject of use of force. They are often central parts of law enforcement agencies' use of force policies. Various criminal justice agencies have developed different models of the continuum, and there is no universal or standard model.

Chapter One

Raising the Bar: Education, Training, and Screening

In the vast majority of police departments and sheriff's offices in America today, a young man or woman can drop out of high school, get their GED, go to a police academy, and be hired as a patrol officer or deputy. Once they hit the street, they'll have more authority over an average citizen than the judges who've been trained and educated for years: Officers deal with the public at large. Judges, not so much.

In 2013 (the most recent year in which the U.S. Bureau of Justice Statistics released the data), the average length of police training nationwide, including field training, was just shy of eight months. About the same amount of training needed to be a hair stylist or welder. Yet new law enforcement officers – many of whom are really just kids – will often make life-and-death decisions long before their training (much of which happens after they've hit the street) is even complete.

I became an officer for the Augusta Police Department three months out of high school. The only reason I wasn't almost *immediately* on patrol was that my assigned FTO was on his honeymoon. I was probably more mature than most cadets – I'd been working since I was a kid – and I was blessed that my youth and inexperience didn't lead to loss of life or limb. Since those days, I've increased both my education and training exponentially. Which is why I so firmly believe that recruits today need more of *both*.

When I was a police academy director, we used to say, "If you think training is expensive look at *failure* to train."

In my letter to the governor of Georgia following the George Floyd case, I recommended 4-year degrees and standardized training certification for all law enforcement officers, along with extensive background checks and psychological screening.

I discussed all of these things with my panel.

EDUCATION

TOMMIE WALKER

Education is very important. College education, training in a lot of different areas, being exposed to a variety of cultures - all of those things come into play to mold a better officer, rather than just sending a 19- or 20-year-old through the academy and giving them a badge and gun. When you put the rubber to the road, I truly believe that a more educated officer is a much more prepared officer.

HOBART LEWIS:

I don't think it's just about education. I mean, we have a ton of deputies that have two-year degrees, four-year degrees, a master's degrees...those are not the things that are going to get you hired and promoted. What I want to know is what do you do on a professional level? What do you do in service to this community? What are you going to do to serve this agency? What level of professionalism are you displaying? Hopefully, they're honest and humble and want to connect with people and make relationships. That's where it's happening.

TOM THOMPSON

It's just flat out scary that we're hiring kids. In Ohio you have to be 21, but that's still way too young. At that age, you're just not emotionally ready for someone to hand you a gun and say you can take somebody's life or liberty. It's not right. They're just not emotionally ready to handle it, and still totally blind to different cultures. So I think we need some education, some military background, something to get them mature enough.

DEAN CRISP:

I like where you're going with the idea of a 4-year degree, because the root of what you're saying is that if you require a degree, you get a more mature and more balanced, more professional person. But in today's world, a degree don't tell you what it used to. It used to tell you a kid had been away from mom and daddy for four years. Nowadays, they get their degrees online in the basement in their underwear. Hell, it just doesn't mean the same thing.

JOHN WILCHER

I'm all for education. That's one of the things I push here, whether it's education through college or education through training. I've got people here with degrees, but a college degree don't make you smart. All I have is a high school education: I started at the bottom and worked my way to where I'm at today. You can do it without education.

WILLIE BURLEY

Only one percent of police departments require a 4-year college degree. All the studies have shown that college-educated officers are more skilled at resolving problems without having to resort to force, and that those officers generate fewer citizen complaints.

RAMONE LAMKIN

If we require them to have degrees, we have to pay them too. The guys that have degrees and can pass all the background checks and psychological checks go into fields that pay a lot more money, where they don't have to worry about getting killed.

THOMAS SMITH

You have to have a 4-year degree in Minnesota. You can have a degree in another field, like Sociology, but you still have to have your Law Enforcement credits. That's actually hindered some of our recruiting from communities of color. So we're looking at changing that. But I think that education's critical.

WAYNE HARRIS

I support requiring a four-year degree. I also support making it affordable for officers to go back to school and finish their secondary education. A couple of reasons: if we're talking about how to make our law enforcement more respectable, if you will, then having a well-educated force of individuals will serve to help foster trust and respect in law enforcement. The other thing too, is that - just like a doctor has to have a certain level of certification in order to perform surgery - there's an argument that can be made that law enforcement is the same type of situation, where you want people to be as perfect as possible, as well-educated as possible, if we're going to place that kind of responsibility into their hands. Especially if it's going to help to improve that relationship between law enforcement and the citizens we serve.

CHARLES PRESCOTT

I actually started law enforcement my last semester of college. So I came with the 4-year degree, and now I have two master's degrees to go with it. I'm big on education. Also big on experience. But you can be the most-educated person and still be a bad cop, just like you can be the least-educated and be a good cop.

JERRY BLASH

I think education is part of it, but not all of it. Training is a bigger deal to me. Like Charles said, you can have all the education in the world but if you if you're not trained right…I mean, a rocket scientist won't necessarily make a better cop than a fast-food worker. I've supervised officers that had bachelor's degrees but couldn't write a complete sentence.

JIM MANFRE

I think that immaturity is one of the biggest factors. I never hired anyone who was under 22. We went after military vets and had an agreement with the Department of Defense that we would hire as many vets as they would send out. If they did get called up, if they had reserve commitments, we would allow them to serve their commitments and their job would be there when they came back. So we had a lot of success bringing in military veterans, who have already received training and had maturity and had been around diverse people. College is not a cure-all, but again, it allows you to socialize and allows you to meet people different than yourself.

STANDARDIZED TRAINING

WAYNE HARRIS

That's sort of the mindset, to establish those standardizations that agencies would seek to achieve. I think CALEA eventually fell apart for some agencies because it was very, very expensive to accomplish. So yes, I think we do need to establish criteria or standards for agencies to operate under. We have to make it cost effective so that they'll participate in it and we have to make it such that there's a benefit to them for doing it, like tying it to grant funding.

THOMAS SMITH

Minnesota was the first state to go to the POST system. You have to maintain your license, you have to go to training, you have to get a certain amount of credits every three years or they'll yank your license. I think that could be standardized throughout the country as well.

EARLE MARSH

I think we need to have some type of standard. However, it's like any other policy, you don't want to put it in a box. Not every standard that applies to New York is gonna work in Georgia or South Carolina.

JIM MANFRE

I think accreditation is…I wouldn't say it's outmoded, because it gives you an opportunity to retrain your deputies on your policies and procedures, and it's a good exercise. But it's not always reflective of whether your agency has a good rapport with the community. How do you measure that?

JERRY BLASH

I think training needs to be more intense, more realistic, and extended, no matter where you are. In the state of Georgia, it takes over 500 hours to be a nail technician, but only 408 hours to become a cop. I feel like the police academy was too easy and too short. And I left there with too many questions in my head about what I can and can't do. So I feel like the police academy just needs to be longer and more in depth.

BACKGROUND CHECKS

EARLE MARSH

I think background investigations are a must. I think you should know what you got coming in the door. And I don't think bad apples should be able to jump from department to department.

HOBART LEWIS

I think we can do a better job at background checks so that we're not passing around bad officers from agency to agency. Our police academy is centrally located in Columbia, so every officer in South Carolina goes to one academy. We report misconduct violations to the academy, and they're part of a reporting system between academies and certification programs nationwide. Which keeps a bad officer from possibly being hired at another agency, not only in this state, but in another state within the system.

JOHN WILCHER

We do a very, very extensive background check. After we've run a check, I can tell you what color pants you wore when you were three years old. That's how thorough we are.

WAYNE HARRIS

The background investigation in Rochester is very extensive as well. I actually had to hand the questionnaire to my father because I didn't know who he was renting from or what job he was working when I was born.

I think we have to balance it against what we're asking the police to do. Do they need a top-secret security clearance? No, I don't think they do. But I do think it needs to be extensive enough to determine whether or not they are of good character enough to actually serve in this industry. That can be challenging, and it's also costly to engage in that kind of investigation. But I think it's necessary.

The other thing that I'm very, very much in support of is the legislation that's being proposed right now that says if you get fired from my agency, you can't go over here and be hired into another agency. That's critically important.

PRE-EMPLOYMENT AND ONGOING PSYCHOLOGICAL EVALUATIONS

EARLE MARSH

I think we should do at least a little mental evaluation prior to employment. Not everyone's cut out for this job, okay? We did away with the psychological exam for a short period of time at one point, just because we had slots to fill. That cost us more than it was worth.

As far as ongoing evaluation: You know as well as I the things we see on this job, and they're not things that can be talked about to just anybody. Sometimes it helps, to use the old police term, "to go see the wizard." To talk it out with a peer who knows about this stuff.

HOBART LEWIS

Major Ty Miller who works here got with a psychiatrist and started our wellness program. She did a tremendous job setting that up, and we've helped about 80 deputies in a year. I think it's going to be a model nationwide, to be honest. We've helped our deputies deal with alcoholism, drug abuse, depression. We make it mandatory that some of our people – like those investigating crimes against children, who are constantly dealing with child abuse and pornography – periodically talk to someone. I was so proud and pleased to really get inside that program and see how many people we've served.

JIM MANFRE

We had all of our deputies - and employees, for that matter – complete the MMPI psychological tests. It's not perfect, but it helped. We had several chaplains, and I made it very clear to people that our chaplains were there for their benefit. I think there's a huge place for faith-based programs in law enforcement.

We also had an Employ Assistance Program, where our officers had access to a psychologist 24 hours a day, seven days a week, if they needed to talk to someone, and we paid that bill.

You know that in this job we witness some things – car accidents, homicides, and so forth – and we tend to compartmentalize them. You can't go home and talk to your wife because you want to maintain some calm and peace for your family. So you need to be able to have some, you know, pressure relief for events.

THOMAS SMITH

I'm a little hesitant on the psychological tests like the MMPI because I learned some things when I was still chief in St. Paul. We're very diverse in Minnesota – we have large populations of Asians and Somalis – and there are cultural factors which play into psychological testing, particularly with one-on-one exams. Asians, for example, consider it disrespectful to look someone in the eye, and they often smile when they're uncomfortable or feel threatened. So they were failing the psych exams at unbelievable levels. I think that psychological testing could perhaps better reflect the communities we serve.

My biggest thing right now is mental health of officers. We all have some baggage we carry, and in our era we were told to carry the baggage, that any kind of employee assistance or anything like that was a sign of weakness. And it's been a stigma in our line of work that's come back to bite us in the ass.

WILLIE BURLEY

We need psychological evaluations *and* better background checks. An officer should have the mindset to be able to do this job, and to remain clear and focused.

Chapter Two

Trust, Transparency, and Body Cams

We often hear the phrase "bad apples" used in discussions about law enforcement in America today, often by defenders of the police. "Don't judge us by the actions of a few bad apples." While it's true that the rogue officers who capture all the headlines are by no means representative of law enforcement as a whole, we often lose sight of the fact that the *original* phrase is *"One bad apple spoils the bunch."*

Our law enforcement "bunch" is in trouble, with the rot spread not by the offending officers themselves but by the rancid and rampant air of mistrust which their actions foster within the hearts and minds of the public we serve.

One of Sir Robert Peel's "Principles of Policing" is *"To recognize always that the power of the police to fulfill their functions and duties is dependent on public approval of their existence, actions, and behavior, and on their ability to secure and maintain public respect."* I'm not one to mess with perfection, but I believe Sir Peel could have simply said, "*Without trust, there is nothing.*"

Transparency is a key building-block of trust. In law enforcement, there is no greater tool for transparency than body cams.

CALEA has over 460 standards which have to be met by law enforcement agencies in order to achieve accreditation. Body cameras for all officers isn't one of them. This is 2020, and that's insane.

I talked about all of these issues with my experts.

JIM MANFRE

There's so many law enforcement officers and managers who are against body cams, which drives me insane. There is nothing negative about body cams. I was having some problems trying to implement them in Flagler County when Daytona Beach had an incident where a former NFL football player was holed up with a knife to his girlfriend's neck. He was plunging the knife into her neck when a deputy shot him. Didn't kill him. Obviously the first thing that was said was that it was excessive use of force. Body cameras exonerated the deputy in one week. There's no doubt in my mind that body cameras work…you know, with proper procedure: you don't turn that body camera off. If you do, you're fired.

EARLE MARSH

You have to build what I call a "bank of trust." I think we should tell the public what we do a show them what we do. I don't think we should keep any secrets. However, don't let transparency be a weakness. If you're doing it all for the right reasons, transparency is not a problem.

JERRY BLASH

Transparency is a big thing. We've got to get the facts out there before the media does. Because whatever comes out first becomes the truth.

JOHN WILCHER

We've got to be transparent. Every one of my officers on the street, every one of my sergeants and above in a jail, has a video camera. And then I have 1240 cameras in my jail, everywhere except for the restrooms. So you got eyes on everything that everybody does. And I have a Citizens Advisory Group that comes in once a month and brings me problems from the outside.

CHARLES PRESCOTT

We haven't been transparent enough about teaching the public what we do. We don't want to shoot people. But we don't open up about that stuff.

TOM THOMPSON

Ninety-nine times out of a hundred, body cams have kept us out of trouble. I don't think there's as much a backlash against using body cameras as whether the jurisdiction can afford it. Can they fit it in their budget? As we're all aware, it's not the cost of the cameras as much as it is the cloud storage. And I think that's really where it's at. In Ohio, I believe Mike DeWine is coming out with a plan that by 2022 or 2023 everybody's going to be required to have body cameras.

WAYNE HARRIS

We have adopted for a long time a sort of a closed-ship mentality where we don't give out some information because people don't need to know that. The reality though, is that nature abhors a vacuum. And that vacuum is going to get filled, and we've allowed it to be filled by television crime shows - which has been some of the most successful programming since television has been here – and movies, books, and music. And the impression, or the misperception, that it's given is what has become the norm of knowledge for people in the United States. If you ask people if they know about policing, they'll say, "Of course I know about policing: a crime happens, ten minutes later they arrest someone, 25 minutes later he's on trial, and before the show's over he goes to jail."

So I think body cameras for law enforcement use are critically important. And I think they should be used routinely across the country. There's some challenges with the body cameras that are out there right now, partially because in some ways the technology's still very much in its infancy. And the amount of data that you capture digitally is very, very, very difficult to store or to pay to have stored. There's two ways that an agency can do it: they can either store the data in house, which is what Rochester chose to do, or you can third party it out and pay unbelievable amounts of money for the storage on a yearly basis.

Those challenges set aside. body cameras have offered us the opportunity to get at least a better perspective of the interaction between the police and citizens on a daily basis. I know they're not very trusted by police unions. They're very, very aware that the inadvertent capturing of officers talking amongst themselves, and maybe being a little bit more free with their thought process and with their language, places their careers in jeopardy. But I don't think that concern outweighs the benefit that comes from having more information available to us as an industry to determine whether or not what an officer did was proper or improper.

DEAN CRISP

Procedural justice is based on two things: it's based on law, but it's also based on trust. Trust is a bit more difficult to develop and execute than law because laws are black and white, and trust is not. So there's a false narrative, in my opinion, of believing that video creates trust. If you can't believe what a person tells you, and you have to have video evidence of it, you're both screwed. You can't convince someone if there's no trust. I don't give a shit who it is. There's no silver bullet.

THOMAS SMITH

Everything's about trust. If you lose the trust of your community, you've got big problems. And that's all about transparency. If you're in uniform - or wearing your badge and gun - and some kid comes up to you while you're having lunch, you've got a unique opportunity there. Some cops will discourage that kind of thing, just because they don't want to be bothered. But that's a great moment to put a deposit in that "bank of trust" Earle mentioned, and to make a lasting impression on not just that kid but the parents. It's transparency, and it builds trust.

Chapter Three

Too Many Chiefs in the Kitchen: Jurisdictional Issues

I t's often said we are a nation of law. We have a *lot* of laws. It can also be said that we are a nation of law *enforcement*: In the U.S. today, there are nearly 18,000 law enforcement agencies. 18 *thousand*. This includes federal, state, county, and local police departments, but *doesn't* include campus police (who often have full arresting authority) or private security firms.

National standards, as we discussed in chapter one, could go a long way toward ensuring that law enforcement agencies nationwide are "on the same page." But is the sheer number of agencies *itself* a problem?

Our panel of experts weighed in:

JIM MANFRE

I grew up in Fort Lauderdale for a portion of my life. In order for me to go from my dad's house to the beach by car, I used to go have to go through four or five police departments. So Broward County basically consolidated all those small police departments. I think in Dallas they folded 20 police departments into the sheriff's office. What happens is you have less administration, less people butting heads…because unfortunately what happens the more you cut up the law enforcement pie, the more everyone has to have the same toys and compete with each other. And when situations occur that require some sort of coordination, it's like herding cats. So I am for consolidation.

EARLE MARSH

When it comes down to the rubber meets the road, we as law enforcement are gonna do what's right for the greater good. No matter where we're at, on vacation or whatever. A lot of the jurisdictional issues that we have really comes to "the squeaky wheel gets the most grease." So once you give people the opportunity to use that as a tool of leverage, that's where you run into problems.

WILLIE BURLEY

Overlapping jurisdictions should be able to communicate with each other to share and exchange information, news, and ideas. Sometimes we have to swallow our pride and remember that we're all here to serve and protect our community and citizens.

TOM THOMPSON

I've often thought of regionalizing police. I think it's cheaper, and that you draw a more consistent policing picture for the community. The Dayton area might have 20 suburbs, with each one policed a little bit differently. So the expectations of your citizens depending on which suburb they're in changes. I do think it would be more consistent if it were standardized, if you had like a Dayton regional police force and a Cincinnati regional police force. I definitely think that would be better, for the community. Where that's problematic goes back to the politicians, and they all want control of their own city and to answer their own constituents. So if the constituents are in a nice suburb, they want their specific policing done a specific way. It's not equitable. Yeah, I'm a fan. I'm a fan of regional policing, consolidation, whatever you want to call it.

HOBART LEWIS

We don't have any jurisdictional issues here to speak of. I do have seven other municipalities inside Greenville County, seven other chiefs. They're really small agencies, 30 or 40 people, but we help each other out.

DEAN CRISP

I don't think that jurisdictional boundaries are the problem; I think the unwillingness to work together is the problem. Jurisdictional boundaries don't matter to crooks, that's for certain. I think the only people they really matter to is cops, and when the leader of an organization gets overly concerned with jurisdictional matters, that's a problem. I like towns determining what kind of police force they have. I do like national standards on major things that we probably should all be on the same page with, like use of force, police chases, professional conduct, and hiring.

JOHN WILCHER

We have city police and county police, seven municipalities and a sheriff here. I try to work with all of them. I don't try to get in their lane, they don't try to get in my lane. And I think we have a good, important relationship.

Chapter Four

Guardians, Warriors, and Servants

Early on in my career, I came to the conclusion that most police officers fall into one of two camps: crime-fighters or social workers, and that the predilection toward one or the other isn't something which is taught, but is ingrained in the character of each of us long before we pin on the badge and strap on the gun.

It's often the reason we get into this business in the first place.

I've always been proud to consider myself one in the latter camp. To me, fighting crime, "catching the bad guys," is a vital part of protecting the public I serve, but what really brings me satisfaction is helping to create an environment which can lift our at-risk population from the sad cycle which leads them to commit crimes in the first place.

In law enforcement circles, this crime fighter/social worker dynamic is often referred to as "Warrior vs Guardian." It's an important topic, and I believe at the crux of many of the issues we face today.

I asked my panel about it.

DEAN CRISP

A guardian is a person who will find the right services for you. A guardian is a person who cares beyond just saying, "I'm gonna lock your ass up." One of the biggest problems with law enforcement is that every freaking cop is taught in the academy that they can arrest their way out of any stupid f---ing situation.

But you can't be a social worker because this job doesn't allow you the time to be a social worker. What it does allow you the time to do is to be sympathetic and empathetic, to get the right people who can help along that path. If you start trying to be a social worker and a police officer, it's very difficult to do. Because, I mean, when do you drop them? Social workers continue that process. A guardian just puts you in that process.

We're looking at reform from the wrong standpoint. We're looking at reform from individual-based incidents: use of force, chases…you know, all those things that we're talking about. But we really should be looking at reform from the holistic view that cops should be guardians first. Right now they're warriors first. When you've got somebody who walks out with a sword drawn, well, he only knows one thing. It's like giving a little kid a hammer - he sees the entire world as a nail.

HOBART LEWIS

I think it's definitely a combination of both. I think people have to know that you have that warrior instinct in you and it's willing to come out when it needs to. I heard somebody say a long time ago, "Don't mistake my kindness for weakness." But I do want to be a guardian. I want to be a good steward of the faith that the citizens have put in me.

WAYNE HARRIS

If you'd asked my wife whether she wanted me to have a guardian mentality or a warrior mentality while I was working the streets, she'd tell you all day long, "I want that warrior mentality because I want you to come home at the end of the day." But police officers are human beings. They have families, they have emotions, they have psyches that get bruised and have to adjust to all this stuff.

So my best answer is going to be this: I used to tell my officers that if necessary, use just enough force to effect an arrest. But if an individual is seeking to hurt you, or fight you to the point of hurting you, then you use whatever force is necessary to get that to stop. That means that there are occasions when police officers have to embrace a warrior mentality, because they want to go home at the end of the day.

The problem, though, is that if every single interaction is based on that warrior mentality, I'm not doing the service to my community. I'm also not functioning efficiently as a police officer, because the majority of what an officer does on any single day - and I don't care where it is, I've talked to officers from all over the world - is conversational interaction with people that doesn't require a warrior mentality. So the guardian mentality should be the norm. It should be the default, if you will.

TOM THOMPSON

I think you have to have both. And I think we have to train with a balance. We had a situation up in Dayton recently, an active shooter in one of our bar districts. A guy had an automatic rifle and was just mowing people down, and officers responded immediately and killed him. The average guy off the street can't do that unless they have a warrior mentality. The opposite is the guy at the Parkland school shooting, who's hiding outside and afraid to go in while all these kids are getting slaughtered. And that's a problem. That's because he didn't have a warrior mentality.

So I think we don't do active shooter training without also incorporating de-escalation training, and also incorporating training that touches on humanity.

EARLE MARSH

Guardians every single day. Warriors when it counts.

THOMAS SMITH

I teach this in FBI leadership training and in local Quantico police training as well, and I go one step further: The servant mentality. I believe we're all three, and I don't believe you can separate them. Back in the early 90s a gang member came from California to Minnesota to make a lot of money and tried to shoot and kill us. You know, I think we were warriors there. But in tracking that guy down, we were guarding the public as well. What I believe is that we're Peace Officers.

JIM MANFRE

The irony is that law enforcement is 99% words. Not fighting, but words. Now we have to have all this military crap.

My brother's a retired Army lieutenant, my son's an ensign on a carrier out of San Diego. They didn't even teach *them* to be warriors. They taught them to be managers of people. So this whole "warrior mentality" makes no sense and should have never existed. It's not successful.

Chapter Five

Strained Bedfellows: Politics and Policing

P olitics in America has never been as divisive as it is today. It's also never been so intertwined with law enforcement, most often at the expense of the public we serve. Politicians, while – in my opinion – mostly honorable and well-intentioned, rely on votes and have to cater to the whims of an often un- or mis-informed public. And most of them (politicians and public alike) don't have the first clue about law enforcement.

I know what you're thinking: As a sheriff elected by the voters of Burke County, I'm probably more of a politician than most in this business. An understandable assumption, but not reflective of reality. I rely on votes to keep my job, but – once elected – I don't really have to *answer* to any politicians. Something which can't be said of most other law enforcement leadership roles.

I think about things like *truth* and *right and wrong* before I think about politics. Always have. When I was with the Augusta Police Department,

I was one of the few willing to confront the mayor about injustices within the department. If I hadn't notified the press about the meeting, I probably would have been fired. I didn't care. And the issue was resolved to benefit of hundreds of my fellow officers. (I talk about this more in-depth in *Not Here To Be Served*).

Nor did politics enter into my thinking in June of 2020, when I went on CNN and said that, in my professional opinion, the Rayshard Brooks shooting in Atlanta was "100% justified." (My panel and I go into that more in-depth in the *Use of Force* chapter). You may hate me for my opinion (many folks do), and I'm sure it'll be used against me when I run for re-election in 2024. I don't care. That's *all* politics. Truth is bipartisan.

Unfortunately, in today's climate, it's not necessarily politically expedient to proclaim support for our profession. "Defunding" is today's catch-phrase. As disheartening as this is (and the goal of this book is to hopefully help *change* that climate), politics affects policing in a multitude of other, perhaps less-talked-about ways. Some of which I discussed with my panel. And, of course, we talked about defunding too.

JIM MANFRE

There's no politics in firefighting, right? Everyone knows how to fight a fire. Whether it's Flagler County, Florida, Burke County, Georgia or Paris, France, we fight fires the same way. There's no politics about ambulances: EMTs are trained the same way all over the world. Same with disaster preparedness: there isn't any ideology involved with a hurricane preparation, and I've had six hurricanes to deal with in my career. No ideology there. When it comes to basic policing, somehow we inject ideology and politics into it. It's absolute nonsense, and a bad way of doing things.

THOMAS SMITH

I'm old enough to have seen things go both ways in our profession, and I know you've got a few decades as well in the profession. I've watched politicians that have been very supportive of our profession, and then I've gone to where we are right now. So I've watched that pendulum turn. Most times it's right in the middle.

I've done a lot of work with politicians. With the previous administration, I spent a lot of time in Washington D.C. and with the United States Attorney General and the Department of Justice, trying to bring together communities and to get politicians to listen to our voices. Because I think, as we both know, that if you have politicians trying to change policy for law enforcement – something they have no expertise in – it hurts our profession and more so it hurts our young deputies and officers. I think that's a recipe for bad things to happen.

When we can work at the local, state, county, and federal levels together, when they can hear our voices – like with your letter to the governor – then we can at least have that dialogue and maybe come to some successful conclusion. Silence is deafening.

EARLE MARSH

This is the way I relate politics: "Poly" means *many* and "tics" means *bloodsuckers*.

Every time we get new politicians, they all have new ways of doing things. And it comes down to buzzwords, like "defund."

Police have become more reactive than proactive due to a lack of people wanting the job and a lack of qualified people to hire for the job. To me, politics play a big role in that, because they hold the purse strings.

In most cases, you're going to be here longer: I've outlasted most of the politicians.

TOM THOMPSON

I've really found that most politicians just want to get elected again. Sometimes when they get involved, it can be healthy. But sometimes it's not healthy because they're just looking at the citizens as votes, and don't see what their real needs are. So it's a kind of a mixed bag.

WAYNE HARRIS

What I used to tell my officers is this: There's always going to be politics surrounding what we do. Whether it's governmental or community, there's a certain aspect of politics that will always be in play, that we as officers don't necessarily have any control over. We can't take a direct hand in it because it'll violate a general rule that prohibits getting involved in political activity. So it's important for them to be able to compartmentalize something and say, "This is the politics that's happening right now."

Regardless of the politics, we still have a job to do. We still are answerable to the community that we serve. So it's a difficult challenge, but politics does impact us just as much as the physical, psychological, or emotional stress does.

HOBART LEWIS

Obviously, I won an election and that is the political process. And we know how important constituents are, but people call you when you win and say, "Hey, I need this because I voted for you," and it's difficult to explain to those people that you're not owned by them. It's not how this works. So you certainly try to stand your ground.

JOHN WILCHER

When I first took office in 2016, I met with the county commission chairman. I met with the county manager and the county attorney along with my attorney and my chief deputy, and I said, "Look, people, I'm gonna work with you. You set my budget, I'll spend my budget." I said. "But don't call me up and say, 'You need to run over there to Al's house, he's got a barking dog.' I'm not that kind of person. I work for the people. I don't work for y'all."

The county sets my budget, but they don't tell me how to spend it. And we've got along real well. The thing about it is, you and I know how to run our offices, and it's kind of a relief that we don't have to put up with all the BS the police department does. The police chiefs have to deal with the mayor, the city council…lots of politicians.

BILLY HANCOCK

Law enforcement should be fair and impartial and serve without political patronage. We distance ourselves from the vicissitudes of politics as much as we can because we must protect and serve *everyone*. Politics impacts multiple facets of policing. Politics can heavily influence the duties of officers, formal policy, and even take away officer discretion. Political affiliates are goal-oriented, and law enforcement is not a platform that should be used to further a political agenda. There is no place for one-sided politics in policing, prosecution, judication, criminal justice, or due process. Our duty is to protect and serve the people, not protect and serve as a politician sees fit. We are here to live up to our nation's founding ideals and protect the rights of all persons. Any law enforcement official running for office should be non-partisan, especially in the case of a Sheriff.

ON *DEFUNDING*

DEAN CRISP

It's a knee-jerk reaction to liberals who believe that taking police money somehow minimizes the police. It's not a real policy. It's a punishment for police because we've seen these actions across the country, and these weak-ass city managers and council members just play to the loudest voices.

If they take 50% away from the police, we'll answer 50% of the calls. How does that work? Which calls do we ignore? It's not a real policy.

EARLE MARSH

When people talk about defunding, what they're really talking about is taking money from the police and giving it to other agencies better equipped to handle those issues. So the police have less to do. Hey, man, if you can take the burden of us having to respond to, say, a dog running loose, and take the money we would've spent answering that call and give it to a dogcatcher, I would be happy with that.

JIM MANFRE

I don't even know what that means, right? To be honest, I think it's one of those words that encourages people to fight with each other rather than compromise with each other. I like to use the word "reimagine" rather than "defund."

RAMONE LAMKIN

That's a very dangerous word and you're going down a very slippery slope when you talk about defunding the police. And I do agree we need resources for mental health, but I don't think we take resources from the police to do that. As a matter of fact, we need to *add* resources. Make it so we can offer retirement and pay our officers better.

Chapter Six

Long Arm, Helping Hand: Law Enforcement and the Community

Another of Sir Robert Peel's "Principles of Policing" is *"To maintain at all times a relationship with the public that gives reality to the historic tradition that the police are the public and that the public are the police."*

"Us vs Them" has no place in law enforcement. It's *all* us.

As a young boy growing up in Waynesboro, I was drawn to policing in part because of the way the local cops seemed to be a part of the community. Sure, they had *guns*, but that was to protect us from harm. The rest of the time, they were just there to help.

Throughout my career, I've strived to be a servant of the people, a goal which I believe is reflected in the priority I've placed on community at the departments I've headed up. My Burke County Sheriff's Office has no less than seven programs administered by our Community Services Division, and that's just a small part of the resources we provide. Almost none of that has anything to do with making arrests, but everything to do with bonding and establishing trust with the community.

My wise panel had some great insights:

THOMAS SMITH

When I teach classes to law enforcement, I tell two stories:

Back in the '90s, when I was just a young patrol officer with the St. Paul PD, we were doing a law enforcement recruitment day at the Minneapolis Convention Center. And so they had all these different law enforcement agencies, with St. Paul and Minneapolis side-by-side because we're the two largest in the state of Minnesota. So we've got our big booth set up with the TVs playing the VHS tapes, cops handing out materials, mostly very community-based stuff. And we hear all this noise and yelling coming from the Minneapolis PD's booth. We look over there and – rather than taking our community approach – they're doing these defensive tactics exercises. They've got a guy in a RedMan padded suit getting beat with nightsticks, all that stuff.

Fast-forward to 2014. Former Minneapolis police chief Tim Dolan and I are speaking at this law enforcement program graduation ceremony, and one of the graduates asks Tim about the big difference between the Minneapolis and St. Paul police departments. And Tim said, "To be honest, in Minneapolis we're known for taking over a community. In St. Paul, they're known for being a *part* of it." Brutally honest, but true.

DEAN CRISP

Policing is a partnership. And we are foolish to believe that we move forward without making our communities partners. When you make your communities partners, you create a narrative of trust. When you create a narrative of trust, people are much more tolerant of the things you do in the name of law and order. When there is zero trust, nothing you can do in the name of law and order is going to be sufficient for the people. So we've got to realize that policing is a partnership and it starts with relationships.

JOHN WILCHER

Before the pandemic hit, my calendar was loaded seven days a week. I mean, I was going somewhere at least two or three times a day. And that's all about being transparent, being in a community for the people. Just like I told you when I first met you, these people don't work for me, I work for them.

When I got elected in '16, we had close to 1900 prisoners each day in our jail. Today we've got just over 1200. A lot of that's because we were incarcerating so many people who had mental health issues and just needed treatment. I said, "Look, let's do something with this mental health stuff." So we got together to build a mental health facility, and they get these folks back on their medication and they become productive members in the community.

We'd always rather help folks out than lock 'em up.

RAMONE LAMKIN

We're always out in the community. They just did a news story about some neighborhood cleanup we were doing, and they talked to a guy who said how good it was to see law enforcement out in the community, not in an adversarial role, but more symbiotic. When they see us out there cleaning up their neighborhood, it inspires them to do more and hopefully it makes *them* want to do more. And that's it. We've got to have those one by one, neighborhood by neighborhood, just having a holistic approach. And when it's something we're not able to handle – like mental health and homelessness – we can step up and refer them to the right people.

WAYNE HARRIS

I think we have a disconnect between police and the communities that we serve – distrust going both ways. One of the things I set up as a way of combating this before I left the department is called the Police Training Advisory Committee, where I took as wide a spectrum of people as possible - from those who were vehemently opposed to the police department to those supportive of the police department, and everyone in the middle - and laid out all of our training manuals, all of our rules and regulations, all of our general orders, everything. I asked them to advocate for us in the community when questions about our training and our policies and our procedures came up, but to also make recommendation to us from the community. For me, it was valuable because it created that connection, that bond that's necessary for true community policing to exist. So, you know, we went above and beyond to try and bridge that gap.

JIM MANFRE

There was a time where law enforcement was a local neighborhood guy that would show up when you got into trouble. They were the guys who would call your parents. We got away from that somehow, but were starting to get back to it, I think, before this last wave. Now it seems a lot of departments just want to kick ass and take names. Police have to create a bond with the community – when that gets broken, it never gets fixed.

WILLIE BURLEY

In order to bridge the gap, law enforcement officers need to bond more with the community. We should interact with the public at any public events, church events…even with everyday patrolling. Any kind of positive communication with the community that shows respect, even if it's just walking the neighborhoods and talking with people and business owners. Anything to let them know that we're there for them and concerned about their well-being will help with bridging the gap. I believe it will take a lot of work and building up trust in order for the community to trust law enforcement officers again, but it can be done.

TOM THOMPSON

A lot of these jurisdictions say, you know, "We're going to go set up a tent once a year and we're going to have a cookout and we're going to hand out bling," and think that's really bonding with the community. I don't think that cuts it. I think it's nice, but it's not what's going to really build that trust. People need to see law enforcement working hand-in-hand with the communities to enhance their way of life. It's relationship-building.

One thing I set up was a Community Enhancement Program, where we had officers working side-by-side with members of at-risk communities, doing enhancement projects. No guns, no vests, just team members working on a project: sweating together, eating together, learning about each other's histories. So it's not like these cops are policing foreign territories, but their own neighborhoods. And I think the neighborhoods would have *their* backs too. Because they'd know each other.

Chapter Seven

Use of Force

Use of Force, in the context of law enforcement, is generally described as "the amount of effort required by police to compel compliance by an unwilling subject." The corresponding Peel's Principle is "To use physical force only when the exercise of persuasion, advice and warning is found to be insufficient to obtain public co-operation to an extent necessary to secure observance of law or to restore order, and to use only the minimum degree of physical force which is necessary on any particular occasion for achieving a police objective."

It's this area in which we are the most thoroughly trained, and the training which – on any given day – we're least likely to use. And as rarely as we actually use force, the use of deadly force is – proportionately – almost unheard of. The overwhelming majority of law enforcement officers will never in their careers use deadly force. Not once.

Yet, obviously, the use of force - deadly or otherwise – is an issue which is at the core of much of what plagues agencies nationwide and casts suspicion and mistrust on our profession as a whole. Much of the criticism is justified: I don't know anyone in law enforcement, including my panel, who doesn't believe that. There's also a lot of criticism which isn't justified, fueled by social media and a public prone to coming to conclusions - based only on headlines, memes, and video clips - without bothering to seek a context and truth which might invalidate a pre-conceived narrative.

Every police shooting or use of force is not created equal.

As you probably know, I condemned the George Floyd killing immediately, both publicly and in my letter to the Governor. I did this because it was the right thing to do, and because it was the truth. Less than two weeks later, following the Rayshard Brooks shooting in Atlanta, I also spoke what I believe to be truth, and what I believe to be right, both to CNN and in an op-ed to The Augusta Chronicle: that, based upon training, protocol, and police procedure, Rolfe was 100% justified in using deadly force.

Could the situation have been handled differently? Of course. Hindsight's 20-20. Could Brooks' death have been prevented? Almost certainly. Do training, protocol, and procedure need to be looked at? Absolutely. That's a part of the dialogue now happening across the country and in this book. But that's not the point in this specific case. The point is whether the shooting was justified based upon current law and protocol, and whether the officer had reason to believe that either his life or the lives of others could be in danger if he didn't act. I believe it was, and I believe he did.

As unpopular as my views were (and are), they were later echoed by multiple state-wide and national law enforcement agencies and organizations. That it took them so long to speak up is part of the problem.

I discussed many facets of the broad but vitally-important topic of use of force – including the Rayshard Brooks case - with my panel of experts.

WAYNE HARRIS

The reality of law enforcement is this: Sometimes, bad stuff happens. We are placed in a situation where we have to fight, or we have to rush in and save lives or we have to do something that is physically demanding and sometimes violent. Unfortunately, that's the nature of our country. One of the things I lecture on is our glorification of violence and also our willingness to use violence as a means of expression. I serve on the board of the Gandhi Institute for Non-violence, and I've been sort of dealing with the question of violence for a long time, because it so impacts our industry. If we understand and accept as a society the fact that when bad stuff happens, when violent stuff happens, the first people that are going to rush into that situation are law enforcement, we have to be okay with them, to the degree necessary, using violence. This is the conversation we need to have with our communities.

In many cases, an officer simply can't get a suspect to submit to an arrest without using a pain compliance technique. It just can't be done. One of the ones we use is a strike to the common peroneal nerve cluster, which runs down the side of your leg. Totally non-lethal. But you get 15 seconds of video, and it looks like the cop's beating the crap out of the guy. The public doesn't know about the common peroneal nerve clusters. They just see beating and screaming. As we're talking about how we can repair what's broken, that's what's broke: We've never told people what they're seeing. Until we bridge that gap, we're still going to have all these misunderstandings that occur out there. And so long as we have the negative information or the misinformation, we're still gonna have these problems.

When George Floyd occurred initially, because it was so horrific, FOPs and unions and police agencies almost uniformly said, "Yeah, that's wrong. That's gotta go. There's nothing right about that." But as time went on, they began to circle their wagons and they sort of individualized this one officer and they said, "Well, there's more to it than you understand," and they started releasing negative information about George Floyd. That's a problem. And the fact that they didn't also speak out against the Brooks case is equally as much a problem because it goes back to what I was saying before. We have not gotten to the point where we can talk about the stuff that's happening. I can tell you right now, when the Brooks thing happened, and it was painted with the same brush as George Floyd, my first thought – based upon my experience not just as a cop but as an experienced internal affairs investigator – was, *Hang on a second.* This is a guy that was actively engaged in combat with a police officer, stole his taser, then fired it at the officer, which could have incapacitated him…then there's a gun right there. So the dynamics of the Brooks case were not as cut and dry as the media and everyone else tried to make out.

TOM THOMPSON

I think, personally, that the Brooks case was not a good shoot. I had a long talk with my Trainer and Trainer Supervisor, and it always comes back to "Why did Brooks do that? Why did he fight, why did he run?" I told them to look at it from Brooks' perspective. Maybe he had an outstanding warrant, maybe he just panicked. Maybe he'd just been watching ten straight days of coverage of a white officer killing a black man. Maybe he thought he was fighting for his life.

I don't know. But I think what I saw on the videos would not have been enough for me to okay that shooting. Now do I think that Rolfe needs to go to prison forever? I think that what sometimes the public doesn't understand is just because we might look later and Monday morning quarterback and say he could have done something different, that doesn't mean that he's criminally liable for it.

But I wouldn't have wanted one of my officers to do that shooting. Let's put it that way.

I've often heard the argument that if guys keep getting in trouble for use of force, they're going to be afraid to use it when they have to. I just have never really seen that to be the case. When I took over policing for the Kettering hospital system, I know that nobody had ever been reviewed for any of their uses of force. You had guys throwing punches at mental health patients and things like that. One of the things I did right up front was say: "Okay, you can use force if it's necessary, but you're going to have to articulate it, and it's going to get reviewed. And we're going to be transparent about it." We went from 11 incidents in the first month to 11 in the next six months total.

I think in most cases the guys who use force just aren't as skilled as those who don't. They've got a short fuse and they lack skills. So they just go straight to the Neanderthal thing.

THOMAS SMITH

I was talking with a superintendent the other day about the use of force continuum, and how every department can tweak theirs. I tweaked ours in the St. Paul police department, when we got the electronic control devices, like tasers. I'm old enough to remember those big-ass PR24 batons…I actually taught those. I'd kill myself with one now. The point is, things change, and we'll adjust our training, but we're slower to change how and when we *use* our training.

For the longest time we had the "21-foot rule," where we were taught that an officer facing a suspect with a knife only has 21 feet to draw his weapon and get a shot off before he gets stabbed. And I always thought, why aren't we trained to move *away* from the suspect? Move left, move right? You know, *de-escalate*? We've always been told to move forward, and police have shot a lot of people who didn't need to be shot.

Of course, the use of force continuum doesn't even come into play as often since 'Graham vs Connor.' Now use of force is based upon "what would a reasonable officer do?" I think there needs to be some national standards.

JOHN WILCHER

We let 'Graham vs Connor' be our gauge. When I came in as sheriff, I cut out chokeholds, car chases, pit maneuvers…all that stuff. With the car chases and pit maneuvers, nine times out of ten it's gonna be an innocent bystander that gets hurt. We can just get their tag number and arrest 'em later. And I told my officers that you damn sure don't shoot nobody unless your life is in danger.

WILLIE BURLEY

All incidents of excessive force need to be investigated, and those officers who've broken the law need to be dealt with. We need to eliminate the bad apples.

EARLE MARSH

Our use of force continuum is set by the state, so all of our agencies are kind of using the same standard.

The biggest hesitancy I have with a national reporting system for excessive use of force is that there's so much gray area and ambiguity involved. We get guys accused of excessive force because the suspect said his handcuffs were too tight. But that still goes down as an excessive force complaint. So it's hard to write all the language in there to encompass all the facts.

As far as chokeholds go, I don't think they should be used as a means of *restraint*, but we all know that in a life-or-death situation, anything goes: bricks, baseball bats, hand grenades, whatever you can get your hands on to make sure you go home that night.

CHARLES PRESCOTT

The average citizen doesn't know a good shoot versus a bad shoot. They just know what they see on social media or the news. We've got to be willing to step up and say, "Hey, this is what we did and this is why we did it."

The egregious stuff, like what happened with George Floyd…we've just got to weed that stuff out.

JERRY BLASH

Excessive force, to me, is defined as intentional malice - not just mere carelessness or overzealousness. The malice was obvious in the Floyd case. With Brooks…I can see where Rolfe might have been careless or overzealous. But I can't see that it was malicious.

DEAN CRISP

Somewhere along the line - because of all the violent crime and the drug wars and the gangs – the community just kind of told law enforcement, "You guys need to take care of this." Well, there's an interesting thing when you tell people to take care of something: If you don't hold them accountable to how they take care of it, then when they take care of it, you can't question their means because you told them to take care of it. Now people aren't willing to give us that broad spectrum of authority.

We've been trying to reform for a long time, but the issue kept going silent because years would pass without any high-profile cases of egregious abuse. Now we're videotaping everything, but the public has not gotten used to the fact that what's lawful sometimes looks awful. And so they expect every arrest to look pretty, but that just ain't the case. That's why they don't video executions.

Chapter Eight

Racism

The majority of Americans believe that racism is a serious issue in our country, and within the criminal justice system in particular. How large a majority depends to some extent upon the news cycle, but it's been that way for a while now. Too long.

As I recount in my memoirs, my home county had a "Coloreds Only" drinking fountain in the courthouse until 1984, and it was generally understood that Blacks only went to the county fair on certain nights. (And yes, many in the community called those "N r Nights"). And it wasn't all that long ago that I had to file a discrimination lawsuit to be able to move my family into a White neighborhood. (I won, and it helped pay for our house).

Now I'm the sheriff. We've had numerous people of color in high positions in our local and state governments. It *is* better in many regards. It's just nowhere near *solved*.

Racists can be found in any cross-section of American society. *Human* society, for that matter. That's just how it is.

All of America needs to have a talk.

Every line of communication that's opened, every dialogue that is had with friends, family, or co-workers, helps – if only in the most miniscule of increments. As peace officers and law enforcement leaders, we have to take the lead in opening that communication and having those dialogues, not only among ourselves but with the public we serve. And "in the most miniscule of increments" won't cut it.

I asked my panel about racism in law enforcement in particular and society in general. Which wouldn't be a complete discussion without talking about Black Lives Matter.

JERRY BLASH

Right now law enforcement has this stigma…so many people have this belief that all police are bad based on what a few police officers do. And they can't lump the 99% of us in with the bad ones, just like we can't judge all the protesters based on the rioters. We can't change them until we change us. We've just got to get out there and show them that our jobs are to make situations better and help people.

EARLE MARSH

I will tell you right now, I have never met any officer who's said, "You know what? I'm gonna go kill me a Black man today," or "I'm gonna go kill me a White man today." Ain't nobody wants to do all that. And you know, it's the mistake of police work that we're not communicating that. I can't sit here and tell you 100% that we don't have racist folks within law enforcement, but I don't practice that. And that goes for anybody that I acquaint myself with or surround myself with. I don't approve of that crap.

JIM MANFRE

For me, there's a simple solution to racism: Don't be a racist.

I believe racism is the last battlefield of the Civil War. That's the battle that we never won or even confronted. Yes, we got rid of slavery, but we never ever tried racism: the systemic racism which requires people or influences them to treat Blacks - or any other group - less than equal. I can't believe that Black Lives Matter is even up for discussion. I mean, of course *all* lives matter, but *all* of us weren't slaves, and haven't been systemically discriminated against in every walk of society. If we can't even agree on that, I don't know how we're going to get to this conversation.

We have pressure now to make dramatic changes, not incremental changes: systemic institutional changes in how we relate to each other and how law enforcement relates to the community.

JOHN WILCHER

99.9% of officers who pull somebody over, it ain't because you're Black, it ain't because you're White. It's because you broke the law. We all got to live together, and we can only do what we need to do now to make this world a better world. I could give a damn what color somebody's skin is.

RAMONE LAMKIN

Being a Black man, I've seen a lot of the unfair treatment, and I think that reform is needed in law enforcement and society. I've been pulled over more than once, even when I was in full uniform, because I'm Black. But I was elected to protect the citizens of Richmond County, so all lives matter here.

I think changes need to be made on both sides. Systemic changes, but also changes within our own communities so that this stereotype of the "angry Black man" isn't so cool to Black kids. I think it's gonna take education. I'm trying to teach my own kids not to look at color.

We all have biases, but you can't deal with it until you recognize it.

THOMAS SMITH

Racism is a big deal. We've all got stories of getting pulled over just because of the color of our skin. I drove a nice Caddy back in the '80s, and you know, if you had a caddy back then you were slinging some dope.

I'm 46% African-American and my family goes back to the Congo. My wife's Hispanic, so in my household we have Black, Hispanic, and Native American with a little Irish and Scottish mixed in.

I grew up always being called half-breed and different names and things. So one of the blessings that the good Lord has given to me is to be able to bridge and work with diverse communities. And that's been my strong point. It's the reason I became the chief. It's all about partnerships and relationships.

You have to be able to reach out and work with everybody in this line of work. And I don't care if you're black, purple, yellow…you have to do it. Even when people don't like you, which goes back to Martin Luther King's quote about challenge and controversy. If you don't listen to diverse opinions, then we end up where we are today right now.

TOM THOMPSON

We adopted a young man from Africa over 20 years ago, so I've kind of seen a different view of racism than a lot of White cops, and it's really, really opened my eyes. My son's a retired professional athlete now, but no matter the money or position he had - and still has to this day - I've seen how he's had to deal with a lot of what I would classify as systemic racism. So I've had the opportunity to see that and at the same time be a part of a policing world that sometimes negates the impact that has on people. You know: "This isn't really a big problem, these kinds of things really don't happen." Or "Everybody has the same chance." I've had a chance to see both worlds and been angered sometimes at the way that my son or grandkids have been treated or talked about. At the same time, I think I've been blessed to have a lot of very different opportunities and see the world from a lot of different angles while coming up through the criminal justice system.

One of the big things I think is that police departments are predominantly White, and most of the White officers have a huge blind spot. They don't know what they don't know. They grew up in mostly-White communities, went to mostly-White schools, and have all-White families and friends. All they've ever heard is, you know, that we all have the same opportunity in the United States. So when confronted with something different, it's a complete and total blind spot.

I've had many opportunities to share my perspective with fellow police leaders and officers, and invariably I'll get a call or text the next day from someone saying they couldn't sleep thinking about this stuff. "Does that really happen?" In their minds, everyone's on equal footing.

So a lot of it's not because they're bad guys or bad cops, it's that they just don't really *know* about it, because they've never been exposed to it.

WAYNE HARRIS

Is there a specific problem between White officers and Black people in the United States? Yes. There's a huge distrust about how we have always treated people of color in this country. I teach a course on "Implicit Bias," so of course it's an important issue. We can call it "Diversity Training," it's still the same conversation. There is really research that will indicate that a Black person will be viewed more negatively than a White person will be viewed, and as more of a threat. So there's some very, very ingrained perceptions and biases passed down from generation to generation.

Do I think that all White officers are bad or racist or prejudiced against Black people? No, I don't. That number is probably extremely, extremely small. The ones that are bad get in the news the most because of the way our information cycles work. The negative interactions are what we care about versus the positive interactions that are happening on any given day.

There are over 18,000 police departments in this country, which translates to millions of interactions every single day between the police and citizens, only a fraction of which ever become physical and a smaller fraction of which can be construed as abusive. So statistically, no, there's not this overreaching, overwhelming problem between police and the Black community. But we can't use those statistics as an excuse to not have difficult conversations. If we don't get there, the culture won't ever move beyond where we are right now.

Everyone is impacted by racism to some degree or another. So if we can get people to understand that, and that it's ingrained in every societal structure that exists within the United States, then we can begin to have that conversation. But that's a tough nut to crack.

Chapter nine

Do As I Say AND As I Do: The Role of Leadership in Law Enforcement

From my first real job as a teenager at the Waynesboro Piggly Wiggly (where I worked my way into a management position), through my years serving in law enforcement, I've gravitated toward leadership roles. Not because I've wanted to be a "boss," but because the higher up the totem pole you climb, the better able you are to effect change for the good. You'll find this true of most leaders who have dedicated themselves to their professions, and it's certainly true of the law enforcement leaders we assembled for this book.

I asked them not only how *they* lead, but about the crucial role law enforcement leadership – from FTOs to chiefs and sheriffs to police organizations and unions - will play in meaningful reform.

DEAN CRISP

We have a belief we're going to make a difference in people's lives in a positive way. And part of that is helping them get better. So anytime I can help anybody get better and realize their potential…I always say that the graveyard is full of unmet potential.

When I was a youngster, I developed this thing I called "the do-right test." If you do the right thing for the right reason at the right time in the right way, you generally will pass muster on most decisions you make. The biggest problem is this: If you're going to do something, and you're gonna wait till it feels right, it's probably wrong. Because if you wait till it feels right, it's usually about you. When it's about you, it never is going to be about somebody else. And leadership is always about other people, not yourself. So you can't do that shit.

My first year as chief – this was '91 - we had a police shooting that wasn't a good shoot, and I terminated the officer involved. Believe it or not, this made me unpopular. The public didn't seem to mind that it was a bad shoot – many were like, "Hell, you should've shot the guy sooner." I didn't care. A bad shoot is a bad shoot. It was more important for me to let my people know that I wasn't there to explain their way out of a stupid situation.

Leadership requires pushing the envelope every day, expecting a standard where everybody is going to be at their best. And we wouldn't be where we're at today if that was true. We got to push forward and sometimes it's gonna be tough as nails. Doing the right thing is never easy, but it is still the right thing.

EARLE MARSH

I was taught by great leaders and have walked alongside giants in my profession. And they taught me how to be the person I am today and who I want to strive to be tomorrow. I do this job for the greater good.

Simple as that, the greater good. And we all do this job for the greater good.

I don't think it's leadership or organizations that have failed us. It's our elected officials that have failed law enforcement. Period. The same elected officials that beat us up in the media every single day require us to sit outside their house.

BILLY HANCOCK

I've dedicated my career to serving with honesty and integrity. One must lead by example; I practice what I preach and guide my deputies to do the same.

JIM MANFRE

You can walk into a restaurant and, based on your service, you can tell the type of owner it is. And the same thing with law enforcement. You can tell what kind of chief or sheriff it is by how they're treating the public. Every organization reflects the guy at the top. My son just graduated from Duke and I always stop and talk to the local law enforcement and see how they're doing. And I can tell from their first sentence if they have leadership that knows what they're doing.

We are customer service representatives. In eight years as sheriff, I never had a use of force complaint, never had a single complaint filed against me or my deputies. They knew what I expected from them, which was to treat the public like family. Like you would want someone to treat your mother, a sister, a brother, a father when they got pulled over. I don't give a rat's ass about tickets and all that, I care about "thank you." That's what I want to come out of every interaction – not handcuffs.

You know, a lot of law enforcement is very reluctant to discipline and hold people accountable because, you know, their union contracts or guys getting mad at them for being disciplined. I was not the most popular sheriff, but the deputies who didn't care for me were the ones always doing the stupid things, and they knew I held them accountable. If people do something wrong, you write them up, discipline them, try to get them to improve their behavior. If they don't step up, you throw them out.

This "Blue Line" thing, where we protect the worst of our own…that's such an anomaly, but that small group of people is the reflection the community sees, even though most deputies come to work every day, do their job, and go home. They do it the right way. But those in that small group…that comes down to leadership, too. You have to hold every officer accountable and make it so that they hold *each other* accountable as well.

RAMONE LAMKIN

As law enforcement executives, I think, just like we ask our deputies to hold each other accountable, *we* need to hold each other accountable, and be consistent.

THOMAS SMITH

Leadership is a funny thing, and some leaders don't seem to want to take a stance. Or *lead*. As chief, I struggled at different times with certain rules and regulations, but I wasn't afraid to go out on a limb and tick the mayor off if I felt it was the right thing to do. I wouldn't hesitate to discipline my officers, but I also wouldn't hesitate to praise them, loudly, when they deserved it.

I believe in servitude leadership. I always told my cops as a chief, "You don't work for me, I work for you."

JOHN WILCHER

I tell every officer who comes to work for me: "I give you a tool belt to put on your side. It's up to you to put them tools to use." And I'm not talking about the damn gun. I'm talking about the training, and the resources, and everything you need to have a long career. And I teach them that relationships matter, and that you got to get out in the community if you expect folks to trust you.

WAYNE HARRIS

Even as a sergeant, I always set the expectations I had of my officers. They all knew I worked internal affairs, but knew that if they fell short of expectations, internal affairs was going to be the least of their worries. Now, I was never harsh. In fact, I always insisted on open and frank dialogue and discussion. I would not tolerate people being rude - I didn't think that was necessary under any circumstances, but I valued officers' opinions. I also valued the environment that I established, the culture and the expectations that I set for them for doing the job. You know, we serve at the pleasure of the citizens of our communities. We're stepping in the wrong direction when we adopt this "Us vs Them" mentality, and act like we think we're the ones in charge.

Chapter Ten

Moving Forward: What Does Law Enforcement Reform Look Like?

Over the course of this book, we've discussed what most – officers and civilians alike - believe to be the most important issues facing law enforcement in America today. As part of the discussion, we also touched upon the changes that we feel need to be made.

As I mentioned in the introduction, I laid out some specific changes I felt were needed in my letter to Georgia's governor following the George Floyd murder. You can read that letter in full following this chapter. Many of my ideas – like those on education, training, and national standards - were talked about in-depth, others were included within the context of broader topics. The goal of this book was not just the conversation but to demonstrate that, while we might disagree on some of the finer points, we're all on the same page about the Big Picture.

I asked some of the members of my panel to close with what they believe are among the most important issues, and what steps can be taken *now* to – at the very least – move our profession in the right direction toward regaining the trust needed to effectively meet the needs of the public we serve and protect.

CHARLES PRESCOTT

The obstacle now is trying to repair that relationship between the community and law enforcement agencies. It can be done jurisdiction by jurisdiction, with citizen police, review boards; anything we can do at every level to facilitate transparency and making change possible. We can overcome that obstacle piece by piece.

WAYNE HARRIS

I think organizations like NOBLE and LEAP and the National Sheriffs Association are in a unique position to create the change that we're talking about right now. I think we should be forward thinking and communicate about the things that are prohibiting us from moving forward. And we need to have more conversations like this. The more of our perspective we can get out there on the streets, the better the situation's going to be, and the more productive the conversation's going to be.

BILLY HANCOCK

Policing involves a variety of state and non-state actors. These actors include civil organizations for public oversight as well as law enforcement leaders for internal control and supervision. Executive committees set directions and policies for reform, the legislature provides the legal framework for the reform, and the judiciary reviews the legislation. But it's an ongoing process: we need to look at credentialing, training and technical assistance, the hiring and recruiting process, and dedicated community officer roles.

DEAN CRISP

We've been reforming since Rodney King. That's when you first heard "police reform." But *real* reform needs kind of like an entire cultural revolutionary change, if you will. And that's driven by the people that law enforcement serves.

For our part, we've got to start hiring the right people. If you look at law enforcement today, we are still hiring based upon 1980s and 1990s standards. And the unfortunate thing that those people don't exist anymore. Most police departments aren't even *hiring* as much as *eliminating*. You have so many slots to fill, so you just start eliminating, and fill in the slots with whoever's left.

If I was a chief again, I swear that the first thing I would do is create a hiring unit. Folks who know all about interviewing and vetting. It makes no sense that we'll spend hundreds of hours training and zero hours on the people who will find and hire the kind of officers we need in order to stop this cycle.

And this is another problem with law enforcement now and one thing that I preach a great deal: The police have stopped recruiting their own. Most cops have become mercenaries who don't even live in the jurisdictions they're policing. I don't care who you are, you just care more about the community you're serving when it's *your* damned community.

We've also got to stop spending 98% of our training towards the warrior mindset. The problem with this job is that you spend 98% of the time bored and 2% of the time scared shitless. But you will spend 98% of your prep time for that 2% of the time. There needs to be a hell of a lot more time spent training on ways to *reduce* that 2%.

HOBART LEWIS

We have to take it upon ourselves – because we know what the job entails - to really start opening our eyes and taking a very conscious look at those things we can do different.

Senator Tim Scott here had what I think was a good proposal. And part of his package was we got to hire the best we can get - if you expect the best, you have to hire the best. Whether it's pay increases, tuition reimbursement…if you're going to ask somebody to bring a four-year degree or a master's degree to a law enforcement agency, what are you gonna do to compensate them? And training? If we're going to train them in de-escalation, mental health and awareness, those types of things, we have to allow them *time* for that training, which means we got to add more police officers.

It made so much sense, it didn't get passed.

JIM MANFRE

In my opinion, every single sheriff that gets elected and every single chief that gets appointed should have to go through some national training and sign up for national standards. If they fail to meet those standards, then you pull the federal funding which is attached to that agency. We have to do something to force some more standardization.

Whether it's body cameras, de-escalation, community policing, or dealing with mental health issues among our own...I've implemented all these types of things and they've been wildly successful. There's just so much resistance to things that we know work. Crowding our jails with young people is just the stupidest thing in the world and doesn't succeed.

One of the things we can do to make law enforcement more effective and efficient is to deal with the two elephants in the room: drug and alcohol addiction and mental health issues. Law enforcement is not capable of handling this stuff. We can't mandate treatment; we can't mandate they stay on their medication. There used to be a time, when I started, when there were more social programs to deal with these issues, but politicians kept taking away funding for those, and it all landed in the lap of law enforcement.

If we want to reimagine law enforcement, allow us to do what we're good at. Divert those issues to professionals who can handle that. That's what I did when I was Sheriff. We had an alcohol diversion and drug diversion program. And we had a mental health diversion program. And now our guys are freed up. They're not handling drunks and addicts in crisis – which are the kinds of things that lead to a lot of the use of force incidents.

THOMAS SMITH

We need to have some national standards. I think Congress has passed something to establish a federal police commission that would review all these different things, kind of the next step in the 21st Century Policing. I have two friends involved in that, and I think there's going to be really good things that come from it. But I think also that people like you and me and these other guys are going to have to be champions for our profession. To keep fighting the good fight, whether we're still wearing a badge or not.

TOM THOMPSON

I think a lot could be learned based on the culture and expectations of policing at colleges and universities and healthcare systems. Just the way that law enforcement interacts with the people they serve.

I also believe there needs to be some legislation that limits the power of the unions. Sure, helping people negotiate their contracts is one thing, but helping individuals keep jobs that shouldn't be cops should be legislated out.

TOMMIE WALKER

One of the biggest problems I would say is recruiting: finding officers who are reliable and dedicated. And we have to be more strict – we need to re-evaluate officers and department heads on a regular basis.

JOHN WILCHER

We all want the same thing - to see the right thing done. We need more transparency, we need more training, and we need to make our communities understand that we're here to serve and protect them.

RAMONE LAMKIN

It's gonna take us getting out in the community, getting the trust of our communities, teaming up with our community leaders. Let's have a dialogue and communication with them. When they have complaints, when they have issues, we should take that seriously. We don't need to sweep it under the rug, or to try and cover anything up. We need to let them know that if it's our own who do something wrong, we're going to act swiftly and there's going to be justice.

MY LETTER TO GOVERNOR KEMP

June 2, 2020

Governor Brian Kemp 206 Washington Street Suite 203, State Capitol Atlanta, Georgia 30334

RE: PROPOSED LAW ENFORCEMENT REFORM

Dear Governor Kemp:

Recently, the news reports, demonstrations, and criticisms over use of force issues involving a few law enforcement officers have captured national headlines. As you know, these incidences tend to affect all law enforcement across the country. In fact, they will set us back for several decades.

As discussions on how to effectively reduce the number of questionable incidences of dehumanization of African-American males, cultural contempt for black lives, and complicit behavior by some law enforcement officers, I propose we look globally at ways to mitigate these circumstances. We need those persons within our profession who are in charge at the state and national levels to please consider these preventive measures. They are:

1. Require (over a designated period of time) a four-year degree for

every law enforcement officer in the nation, with those currently serving grandfathered in. A degree does not make one smarter (I am a true example of that), but it gives 18-25-year-olds time to learn, grow, develop, and experience culture, awareness, diversity, and research while affording them some life experiences. Going away from home and being in a collegiate environment helps. Many colleges offer online degrees nowadays; however, the learning is similar as the professor serves as a facilitator to the educational process.

2. Require every police agency in the United States to follow certain certification standards just as we require schools, teachers, doctors, nurses, cosmetologists, etc. to be certified. Similarly, we likely and knowingly would not send our children to a school that is unaccredited, nor hire a lawyer who has not passed a bar exam. States can have additional requirements.

3. Call those legislators and congressmen who we elect to represent us in Atlanta and Washington, D.C. and tell them to create federal legislation to force minimal standards upon law enforcement agencies. For example, every uniformed law enforcement officer should be mandated to have certain training, continuing education, and to wear a body camera. While the camera will not show every angle and answer every question, it is far better than he said, she said. The cameras are usually affordable, but the cloud storage is costly. Perhaps federal dollars can be used to offset those costs. (At the very least, our state should have cloud storage for all Georgia agencies due to the current state mandates regarding body camera footage retention.)

4. Create a federal retirement system for law enforcement officers

to hire, retain and further train the most qualified candidates. (Georgia should step up now as we push for a Federal Option. Florida and South Carolina currently have good examples for Georgia to follow.)

5. Require intrusive and extensive background checks akin to military top security clearances, complete with psychological assessments.

6. Stop making excuses about money when it comes to public safety. Just as international and domestic terrorism are priorities, local law enforcement should be as well. Close down the small law enforcement agencies that cannot afford to do the job employing adequate personnel, training, equipment, and expertise.

7. If you want law enforcement to be respected as teachers, doctors, lawyers, economists, sports professionals, then follow 1-6 above.

The violence and rebellion we are seeing on television are related to many who believe they are not being heard. As the Rev. Dr. Martin Luther King, Jr. said, "The riot is the language of the unheard." We must find meaningful ways to embrace justice, equality, and humanity. Our friends of all races and political affiliation must realize we have protested, rapped, sang, chanted, marched and run marathons without resolve. We must end the contempt for life with a pattern of unfair practices combined with the presumption that all people of color are a threat. As the Negro National Anthem charges, "We need to lift every voice and sing…let it resound loud as the rolling sea".

I charge that we move swiftly to codify the aforementioned practices with a sense of urgency and measured collaboration. I am here to be of service.

Sincerely,

Alfonzo Williams

ACKNOWLEDGEMENTS

olice on Policing was obviously a collaborative effort, and I couldn't have done it without the brave and wise members of my panel – their eagerness to participate I think in itself bodes well for our profession.

Dean Crisp – in addition to be being a panel member – referred me to several of our experts, as did Mikayla Hellwich at *LEAP*. A thousand thanks to both of you!

My editor Ty Hager – with whom I also worked on *Not Here To Be Served* – did another awesome job, and I greatly appreciate his multi-faceted efforts in taking this project from concept to reality.

As any of my panel would tell you, there isn't a single aspect of law enforcement which doesn't require a team – from our Brothers and Sisters in Blue to the family and friends who ground us and provide support and comfort as they shelter us from storms both external and internal. My wife Shirleta and daughters Kiara and Chandler are outstanding examples of this, as are my smart and immensely-talented sisters, Angela, Teresa, Cassandra, and Jennifer. My mother, Miss Rosa Lee Williams, is responsible for pretty much everything that is good in me, and there's no way I'd be where I am now without her.

Finally, I have to thank God, for – without Him – nothing at all is possible.

Alfonzo Williams

September 2020

ABOUT THE AUTHOR

Alfonzo Williams - one of seven children raised in poverty by a single mother - began his law enforcement career with the Augusta, GA Police Department at the age of 19. Promoted to detective at 21, he went on to become a highly-decorated officer, instructor, police chief, and - since 2017 - the sheriff of Burke County, GA.

This is Sheriff Williams' second book. His third, *Murder In Augusta* - a true account of a shocking 1994 murder and the investigation he led - is tentatively scheduled for a November release.

Find more at www.sheriffalfonzo.com.